LEGO NINJAGO
Masters of Spinjitzu

PATH OF A NINJA

WRITTEN BY
BETH LANDIS HESTER

CONTENTS

INTRODUCTION

A NINJA MUST FOLLOW THEIR DESTINY.

The heroes known as the ninja were once ordinary
kids. They ate pizza, played video games, and never
thought about what the future would hold.
But with the guidance of Master Wu, they embark on
a journey to find their true path. With Wu's help, they
are learning to harness their true potential—fighting
for good, protecting all of Ninjago Island… and still
making it home in time for pizza.

A NINJA IS...

NINJA ARE STRONG, stealthy, and skilled at fighting... but that's not all it takes to be part of this elite fighting force! Discover what being a ninja is all about from the friends and enemies who know them best.

NINJA CAN DO WHAT TO OTHERS SEEMS IMPOSSIBLE. THE SECRET IS FOCUS AND DISCIPLINE.

MASTER WU

WE'RE COOL! WE HAVE AWESOME MOVES AND EVEN MORE AWESOME RIDES.

NINJA ARE PESTS! THEY'RE ALWAYS GETTING IN THE WAY OF OUR SCHEMES.

JAY

NUCKAL

SO, YOU WANT TO BE A NiNJA?

MASTER WU KNOWS that a ninja must be ready for danger at any moment, so there is no time to play in his dojo! There is only time for training (and tea, of course). Do you have what it takes?

DEDICATION

Ninja must always be up and ready to dedicate their day to training. Master Wu wakes the ninja every morning with the not-so-gentle sound of a gong. According to Wu, his father—the First Spinjitzu Master—was always up before sunrise and he never complained!

"WATCH AND LEARN, BROTHERS...
ZANE

PATIENCE

At the monastery, a rotating robotic obstacle course imitates an enemy attack. Mastering it requires speed, agility... and a few bumps on the head until practice makes perfect!

FOCUS

Concentration is key to perfecting the quick reactions a ninja needs in battle. Some of the ninja struggle with achieving the right level of focus, but Zane is Wu's star pupil. Or, perhaps he has just gone into standby mode.

TEAM SPIRIT

Training as a group allows Kai, Jay, Cole, and Zane to practice fighting side by side —they'll need to know how to support each other when battling their enemies. It also takes more than one ninja to pull Wu's heavy rickshaw up the mountain, back to the dojo.

WHAT DO NINJA WEAR?

NINJA GEAR IS designed to allow the ninja to perform their most energetic Spinjitzu moves. They have different uniforms for every occasion, but Kai just thinks everything looks extra-awesome in red!

DAPPER GENTS

When the ninja go undercover in a dance competition, their instructor—Cole's dad—gives them these snazzy suits. The ninja aren't impressed.

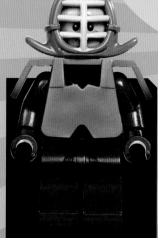

STARTING OUT

Master Wu provides the ninja with this outfit and a rope belt at the start of their training. Zane's snow-white robes and golden Ice emblem reflect his frosty powers.

FLYING OUTFIT

The ninja have gi that show each of their dragons breathing his elemental power. Jay's bright blue robes show his dragon, Wisp, breathing lightning.

TRAINING GEAR

An armored mask and shielded front offer protection when the ninja train. It's too bulky for real battles, but Kai welcomes any barrier from the blows of the training machines.

BATTLE READY

Perfect for fighting, this lightly armored gi has protection in just the right places—on the shoulders and forehead. The silver metal looks great with Cole's black robes.

TRUE POTENTIAL

When the ninja reach their true potential their elemental powers flow through their bodies and enhance their abilities. Zane is the first ninja to unlock this talent.

TEMPLE OF LIGHT

These very ornate, mainly black suits are a symbol of the new, even greater elemental powers the ninja receive in the Temple of Light. Looking flashy, Jay!

ON THE RUN

Cyrus Borg supplies these suits on the eve of a new battle—to disguise the ninja and to help them to fight the Overlord. Kai likes that he no longer has to mess up his hair.

DID YOU KNOW?

A ninja's robes are often referred to as gi. They are recognized across Ninjago Island as the traditional clothing of these brave warriors.

SCHOOL UNIFORM

The ninja take jobs as teachers when Wu opens his academy. They swap their masks and gi for sweaters and blazers for a school trip.

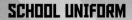

DRESSED TO WIN

When the ninja enter the Tournament of Elements, they pack two outfits. The lightweight, sleeveless robes allow for quick moves in the competition, while their heavy-duty robes are crammed with tools the ninja may need.

WHERE DO NINJA LIVE?

THE NINJA HAVE called lots of places home, but the perfect dojo is very hard to find. ninja need a home that's large enough to train in, well-equipped, and—most importantly for Jay—has somewhere to play video games!

The ninja's original headquarters had great training equipment, but not much space. Cole insisted on creating a strict rota system for the only bathroom after Zane burst in when he was least expecting it!

MONASTERY

DESTINY'S BOUNTY

It took some hard work to transform this old ship into a high-tech flying dojo. After some sprucing up and computer upgrades, it was a sight to behold... until it was damaged in battle.

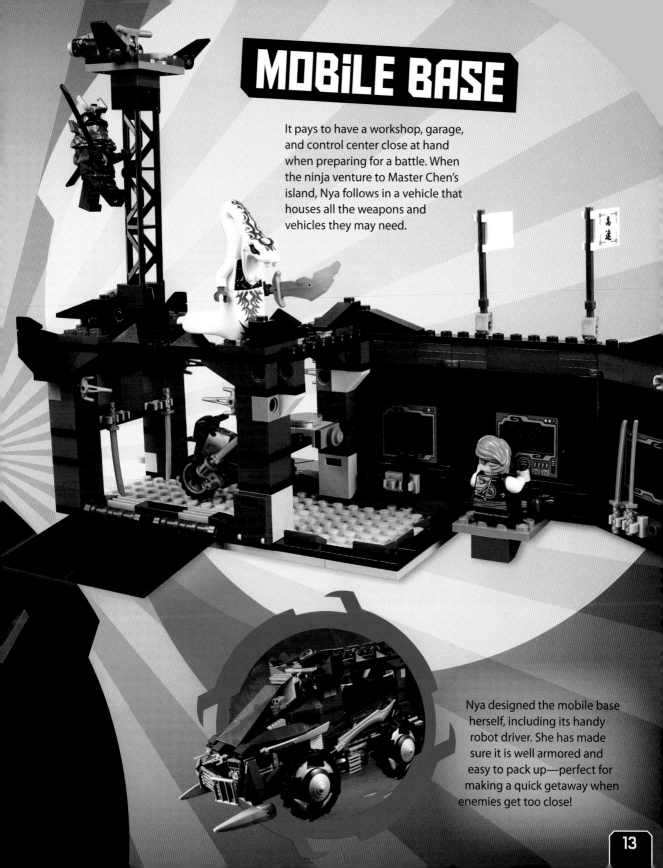

MOBILE BASE

It pays to have a workshop, garage, and control center close at hand when preparing for a battle. When the ninja venture to Master Chen's island, Nya follows in a vehicle that houses all the weapons and vehicles they may need.

Nya designed the mobile base herself, including its handy robot driver. She has made sure it is well armored and easy to pack up—perfect for making a quick getaway when enemies get too close!

Scythe of Quakes

Sword of Fire

Shurikens of Ice

GOLDEN WEAPONS

Created long ago by the First Spinjitzu Master, these weapons were hidden away to stop evil forces using them. They later served the ninja—but their power attracted some unwelcome enemies.

Nunchucks of Lightning

THE POWER OF FOUR

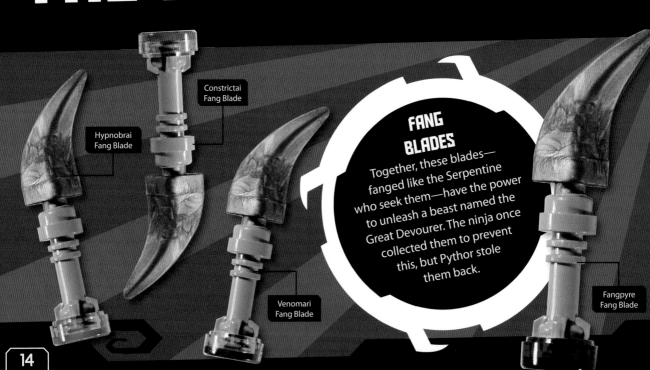

Hypnobrai Fang Blade

Constrictai Fang Blade

FANG BLADES

Together, these blades—fanged like the Serpentine who seek them—have the power to unleash a beast named the Great Devourer. The ninja once collected them to prevent this, but Pythor stole them back.

Venomari Fang Blade

Fangpyre Fang Blade

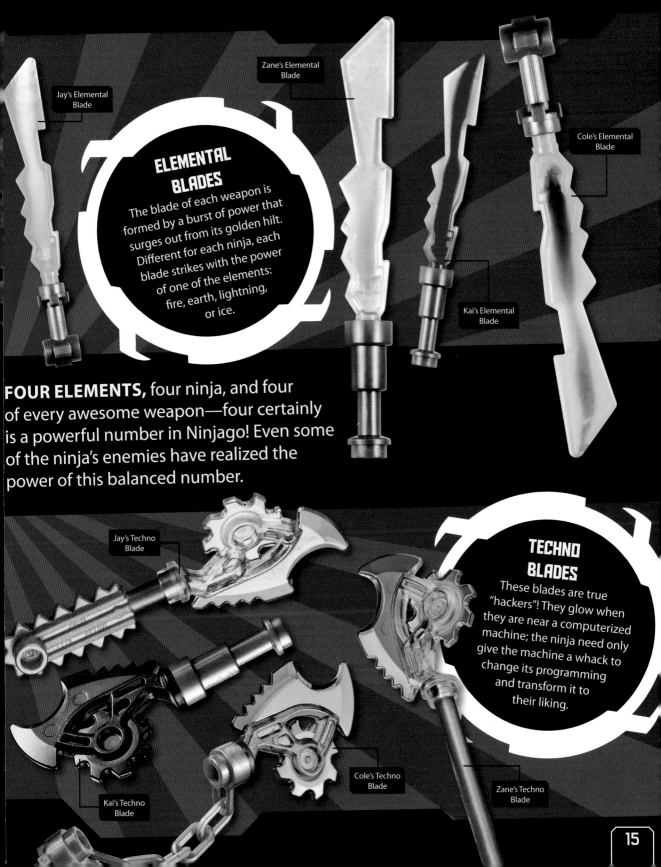

Jay's Elemental Blade

Zane's Elemental Blade

Cole's Elemental Blade

Kai's Elemental Blade

ELEMENTAL BLADES

The blade of each weapon is formed by a burst of power that surges out from its golden hilt. Different for each ninja, each blade strikes with the power of one of the elements: fire, earth, lightning, or ice.

FOUR ELEMENTS, four ninja, and four of every awesome weapon—four certainly is a powerful number in Ninjago! Even some of the ninja's enemies have realized the power of this balanced number.

Jay's Techno Blade

TECHNO BLADES

These blades are true "hackers"! They glow when they are near a computerized machine; the ninja need only give the machine a whack to change its programming and transform it to their liking.

Kai's Techno Blade

Cole's Techno Blade

Zane's Techno Blade

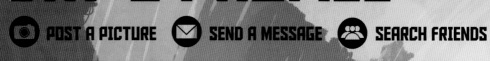

JAY'S PROFILE

📷 POST A PICTURE   ✉ SEND A MESSAGE   👥 SEARCH FRIENDS

Jay posted a picture

Jay Just got a new high score on Fist to Face 2! Don't be too jealous guys, we can't all have my lightning-fast reactions!
Ten minutes ago

Comments

 Lloyd Whatever, Jay. Make way for the Green Ninja! I'll give it a try. Just let me at it.

 Nya Are you seriously still playing that silly game? Don't you have training to do?

 Kai You know I can beat you, Jay!

Jay posted a picture

Jay Fire and ice don't mix well on laundry day. Introducing... the Pink Ninja! Seven hours ago

No comments

Jay updated his location at **Master Chen's Noodle House**, with **Nya.** Yesterday at 18:30

Comments

 Cole Bring home some egg rolls!

Zane posted a picture

Zane It took me a while to compute, but I think Master Wu could be dancing...
Two days ago

Comments

 Nya Who knew Master Wu had moves like that? Looking good, Wu!

 Jay This had to be the funniest moment of the entire year! Master Wu making shapes on the dancefloor. Absolutely classic!

Jay posted a picture

Jay Step 1: Save the day. Step 2: Boogie all night at a victory party!
Three days ago

Comments

 Zane Did someone say party? Computing optimal dance moves.

 Kai Yeah! Make way for the Ninja of Fire... 'cause my dance moves are smokin'!

 Cole If there's cake, I am IN.

 Nya It's party time!

Jay updated his status
Off to develop a few ideas in my workshop. I've had a flash of inspiration! Three days ago

Kai posted a picture of you

Kai The moment Cole got hit with a pie! Five days ago

Comments

 Cole Ha! I'm not the only funny thing in that picture. Check out Zane's apron!

 Zane What is so funny about my flowery apron?

 Jay Dude—are you serious?

 Zane An apron is an effective way to prevent food stains.

Jay posted a picture

Jay Check out the beach style: Awesome shorts, perfectly rumpled hair, just the right amount of blue. The best day EVER! Seven days ago

Comments

 Zane When the weather is pleasant, a day on the beach is certainly most enjoyable.

 Cole Oh, man—do you hear yourself?

 Kai This might have been a good moment for sunscreen... who knew I could get sunburned?

 Lloyd Sure, kick back while I'm off saving the world—no problem!

HOW DO YOU REACH YOUR TRUE POTENTIAL?

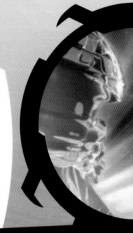

MASTER WU SAYS "In each and every one of us there are obstacles that hold us back. Only when you conquer that fear will your heart be free." Lloyd struggles with this at first, but if his friends can overcome their obstacles, so can he.

FOLLOW YOUR OWN PATH

Cole unlocked his true potential by being honest with his father and telling him he wanted to be a ninja, not a dancer. Once Cole felt confident about his own choices, he earned his dad's respect and some awesome new powers, too.

BE YOURSELF

Jay used to pretend that he was tougher, faster, or cooler than he really was—but Nya helped him realize that he didn't have to pretend: He is already the best version of himself, and that is enough.

DID YOU KNOW?

When a ninja unlocks their true potential, they are able to channel their elemental power better than ever before. The power fills their body and gives them even greater abilities.

SHARE YOUR STRENGTH

Kai was once so determined to be the best, he missed the chance to support his teammates. He found his true potential when he learned that he can succeed by helping others be their best.

ACCEPT YOUR PAST

Zane never knew where he came from, until he discovered the laboratory where he was built. Once he understood his origins, Zane was able to reach his true potential. He used his new powers to save his friends from harm.

DRAGON CARE

THINK YOU COULD take care of dragons for a day? The ninja sometimes have to leave their dragons while they are off fighting enemies, but the dragons still need care and attention. A dragon sitter needs some inside info—and lots of courage—before taking on this fearsome foursome.

ROCKY

OWNER: Cole
ELEMENTAL POWER: Earth
DO: Give him his special dragon snack at 3pm.
DON'T: Forget his bedtime story!

SHARD

OWNER: Zane
ELEMENTAL POWER: Ice
DO: Offer him plenty of refreshing water.
DON'T: Let him get too hot.

FLAME

OWNER: Kai
ELEMENTAL POWER: Fire
DO: Let him out to fly at least once a day.
DON'T: Stand in front of him if he gets the hiccups.

WISP

OWNER: Jay
ELEMENTAL POWER: Lightning
DO: Pet him right between his eyes.
DON'T: Let him watch too much TV.

GREEN NINJA... DRAGON SITTER? THIS WAS NOT IN THE SCROLLS!

WHAT CAN THE NINJA HACK?

CYRUS BORG GAVE the ninja the Techno Blades to help them reprogramme the evil infecting Ninjago Island. The blades also help them make some serious upgrades.

THUNDER RAIDER

With mighty tank treads and rugged tires, Jay's transformed ride storms over rough ground at lightning speeds. For a truly powerful partnership, Cole's Earth Mech can attach to the back to add horsepower and firepower.

EARTH MECH

Cole pounds the ground with each giant step in his fearsome Earth Mech. With built-in missile launchers and stunning speed, the Earth Mech can run, climb, and even join forces with Jay for a team machine that can't be beat.

KAI FIGHTER

An ordinary vehicle becomes this awesome aircraft with a touch of Kai's Techno Blade. In it, Kai can take flight in a blur of red, launching missiles at his enemies as he engages super-speed mode to escape enemy blasts.

NINJACOPTER

Zane flies high in this teched-out copter that's as smooth as ice. Hacked with his Techno Blade, it slices through the air to fight off Nindroids and defend Ninjago City.

X-1 NINJA CHARGER

NINJA ARE TRAINED in stealth—but with a car like this, Kai prefers racing down the highway and getting plenty of attention. This speedster is packed with technical gadgets and a computer system that keeps him in touch with his team.

Missile holders

Headlamps

Shiny metal grille

High-performance tires

DID YOU KNOW?
Kai takes a prototype of the X-1 Ninja Charger to pick up a takeout. He has to leap into action when a Nindroid convoy races past.

Golden detail

Exposed engine

Spoiler stops drag slowing the car down

DID YOU KNOW?
P.I.X.A.L. passes mission details to Kai through the X-1 Ninja Charger's radio system. She can even drive the car remotely.

Golden wheel rims

Wheel spokes cover hidden weapons

Side panels are aerodynamically designed

INTERCEPTOR BIKE
Sometimes Kai is in a tight spot and needs a more compact ride to chase after an enemy. Never fear—the X-1 Ninja Charger has a detachable motorcycle with matching flame details.

WHO ARE THE ELEMENTAL MASTERS?

A NUMBER OF Elemental Masters have arrived to compete in the Tournament of Elements, but the ninja suspect one of them is a traitor. Nya goes undercover to help the ninja get the lowdown on all the crazy competitors.

SHADE
MASTER OF SHADOW

Suspicious Shade stays ou[t of]
the limelight, always nervo[us]
that others are out to get h[im.]

JACOB
MASTER OF SOUND

Blind fighter Jacob can't see what's in front of him, but you'd be surprised what his other senses can tell him.

SKYLOR
MASTER OF ABSORBTION

Skylor can absorb the powers of other fighters—a serious threat considering the company she keeps.

MR. PALE
MASTER OF LIGHT

The power to bend and control light makes it impossible to see Mr. Pale if he doesn't want you t[o.]

ASH
MASTER OF SMOKE

You can't pin down Ash— as soon as anyone gets too close, he disappears in a puff of smoke!

TOX
MASTER OF POISON
This venomous competitor is ready with a dose of poison for anyone who seems like a threat.

KARLOF
MASTER OF METAL
A big brute with a loyal heart, Karlof has fists of steel... and he's not afraid to use them.

TRY HEAVY METAL.

CHAMiLLE
MASTER OF FORM
The mysterious master is hard to spot—just when you think you know what she looks like, she changes form again!

I JUST NEED SOME RUNNING MUSIC!

BOLOBO
MASTER OF NATURE
Powerful but worn from age, this old fighter has the power to control nature.

NEURO
MASTER OF MIND
The ability to read thoughts makes Neuro a dangerous foe—but also a nervous one.

GRAVIS
MASTER OF GRAVITY
Anyone fighting Gravis will soon feel their world turn upside-down as he twists and turns gravity itself.

GRIFFIN TURNER
MASTER OF SPEED
He's not one to wait around for anything—fun-loving Griffin is always rushing to the scene of the action.

Penguin Random House

EDITORS Pamela Afram, Matt Jones, Rosie Peet
EDITORIAL COORDINATOR Clare Millar
SENIOR DESIGNERS Jo Connor, David McDonald
SENIOR SLIPCASE DESIGNER Mark Penfound
EDITORIAL ASSISTANT Beth Davies
DESIGNED BY Dynamo
COVER DESIGNER Stefan Georgiou
PRE-PRODUCTION PRODUCER Kavita Varma
SENIOR PRODUCER Lloyd Robertson
MANAGING EDITOR Paula Regan
DESIGN MANAGER Guy Harvey
CREATIVE MANAGER Sarah Harland
ART DIRECTOR Lisa Lanzarini
PUBLISHER Julie Ferris
PUBLISHING DIRECTOR Simon Beecroft

Additional photography by Gary Ombler

Dorling Kindersley would like to thank:
Heike Bornhausen, Randi Sørensen,
Martin Leighton and Paul Hansford
at the LEGO Group; Radhika Banerjee, Jon Hall,
and Pamela Shiels at DK for design assistance.

This edition published in 2018
First American Edition, 2016
Published in the United States by DK Publishing
345 Hudson Street, New York, New York 10014

DK, a Division of Penguin Random House LLC

Contains content previously published in LEGO®
NINJAGO® *Secret World of the Ninja* (2015)

004-298874-Jul/2018

A catalog record for this book is available from
the Library of Congress.

ISBN: 978-5-0010-1405-8

Printed in China

www.LEGO.com/ninjago
www.dk.com

A WORLD OF IDEAS:
SEE ALL THERE IS TO KNOW